NOAH BUILT AN ARK

RUTH J. WEBB

To order additional copies of this book, contact:
Xlibris
844-714-8691
www.Xlibris.com
Orders@Xlibris.com

ISBN: Softcover   978-1-6641-6514-4
         EBook   978-1-6641-6513-7

Print information available on the last page

Rev. date: 03/24/2021

CONTENTS

INTRODUCTION

This is a true story about a man named Noah. God told him to build an ark because it was going to rain. Noah obeyed God's instructions to build the ark. Because of Noah's obedience, God saved Noah, his family, and the animals from the great flood. God told Noah how to build the ark, every detail, and at the appointed time, when it was time for it to rain, God told Noah to bring his family in and the animals. God told Noah that it was going to rain. Rain was not ever heard of until the ark's door was shut. It rained for forty days and forty nights. This story can be found in the Bible in Genesis chapters 6–9. This is a great story to read to your child at bedtime, or they can read it themselves. This is a great story for any age.

WHO IS NOAH?

Noah was the son of Lamech and Betenos. He was a righteous man. He was a good man. He hated evil. Noah did good in the sight of God. Noah found favor with God.

Noah had a talk with God. God said, "Noah, I am going to destroy all mankind for their corrupt and evil acts."

The world that God created became bad and evil. But Noah was good and blameless in an evil generation.

Noah walked in fellowship with God. Noah made sure that all the animals were cared for. He fed them, talked to them, and made sure they were loved.

Noah had a wife and three sons, Shem, Ham, and Japheth. Noah's sons were good and righteous, and they obeyed their father.

NOAH BUILDS THE ARK

God gave Noah a job. His job was to build an ark.

God said, "Noah, make the ark of gopher wood." So Noah started building the ark as instructed by God.

Noah and his sons put all the wood together. God had given Noah the blueprint on just how the ark should be designed and built. Noah and his sons began to build.

God said, "Noah, make it to have different rooms. The rooms should have stalls, pens, coops, nests, cages, and compartments." God gave him the direct size of the ark. "Noah, the length should be three hundred cubits. It's width, fifty cubits, and the height, thirty cubits. You should make windows for light and ventilation. There should be a first floor, a second floor, and a third floor in the ark. I am going to cause it to rain. The rain will flood the earth. It will destroy all life on earth."

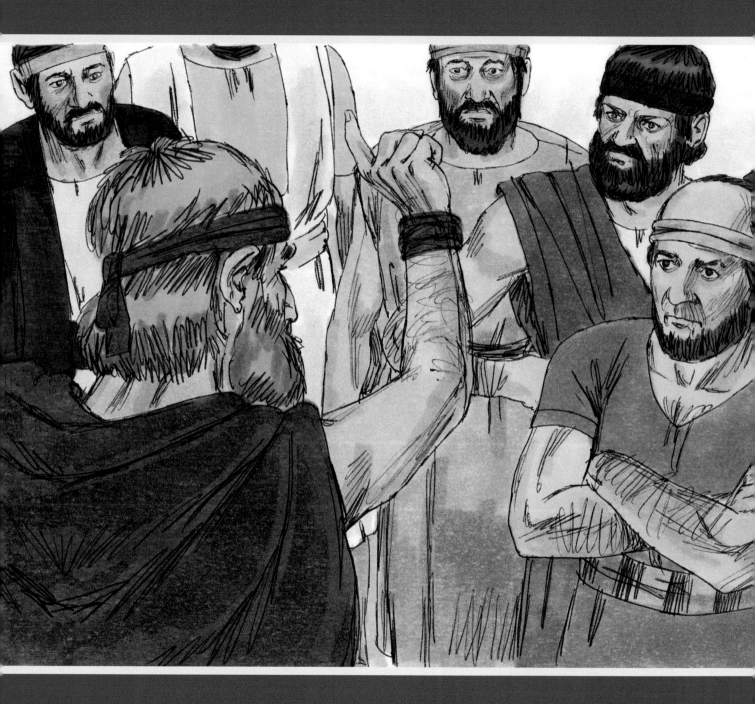

NOAH IS LAUGHED AT AND MOCKED

As they built the ark, the people watched and mocked him. God told Noah that when he'd finish making the ark, He was going to destroy everything man and beast because of evil. So Noah told the people to repent because it was going to rain. They laughed at Noah and mocked him.

Noah and his three sons worked and worked for many years on building the ark just the way God instructed Noah to build it. It had never rained, so the people didn't believe Noah when he told them it was going to rain.

Noah continued to build the ark. He and his sons worked hard day in and day out building the ark, making sure every detail was as God had instructed.

NOAH PREACHES TO THE PEOPLE

Noah would work on the ark and preach repentance to the people. For 120 years, Noah preached the same message: "Repent. It is going to rain." The people just laughed and made fun of him and mocked him. They called him and his sons crazy.

The land where Noah lived was like the desert; the people never heard of rain, nor had they ever seen any such thing as rain. So they felt like Noah was not being honest to them about how it was going to rain.

Noah and his sons continued to build the ark every day and every night; they were working endlessly.

Not one person whom Noah preached to would repent and turn to God.

Noah's three sons got married. They all continued to build the ark. Even though Noah's sons had never seen rain, they believed Noah, their father, and helped him for 120 years to build the ark.

Noah begged and pleaded with the people to repent—to turn to Jesus. But they would not listen. They kept living the same corrupt, sinful lifestyle. Noah continued to preach to the stiff-necked people.

NOAH ENTERS THE ARK

After Noah and his three sons had been faithfully and diligently working hard building the ark God told Noah to build, it was finally completed.

Noah and his family were instructed by God to enter the ark. So Noah gathered his family together and told his wife and their three sons and their wives to enter the ark.

Noah and his family were on the ark as instructed by God. They were now relaxing and enjoying one another's company. They had completed the assignment that God gave to Noah.

God spoke to Noah and told him that only his household would be saved from the great flood. God told him he had seen his righteousness and his obedience.

God told Noah that it was going to rain in seven days. God led Noah every step of the way. Noah did what God told him to do.

THE ANIMALS ENTER
TWO BY TWO

God said, "Noah, of every clean animal you shall take with you seven pair, the male and his female, and of animals that are not clean, two by two, male and female."

God told Noah of the birds of the air, seven pair, male and female. God said, "In seven days, I am going to cause it to rain for forty days and forty nights." Noah did all that God commanded him to do.

Noah and his wife and their three sons and the son's wives all helped to gather the animals onto the ark.

The animals all had their own compartment on their floor of the ark according to what type of animal group they were a part of.

Noah and his family took the animals two by two and seven by seven into the ark. They were all waiting on the ark for the seventh day to come.

There were lions, tigers, and bears on the ark. Horses, wolves, dogs, and cats. Birds, owls, chickens, and hens. Every animal that you could think of was on the ark.

Noah and his family brought on the ark every beast God created—clean and unclean, flying and crawling.

The seventh day had come. God was going to cause it to rain on the earth that had never seen rain and never heard of rain for forty days and forty nights.

Noah tried one last time before he got on the ark to convince the people to turn from their evil and wicked ways and turn to Jesus Christ. He said, "Repent. It's going to rain" as the animals marched on the ark two by two and seven by seven.

GOD CLOSES THE ARK'S DOORS

God told Noah to get on the ark and that he would close the door. God said, "Noah, today it will start to rain." Noah and his family and all the animals were all on the ark as God had instructed them to do.

Noah, his wife, their sons and daughters-in-law, and the animals were now all safe on the ark from the rain that was about to start falling. God closed the door, and no one could open it but God.

IT RAINED FORTY DAYS AND FORTY NIGHTS

Just as God spoke and told Noah that it would rain, the rain began to fall. And it rained, and it rained. The people wanted to get on the ark. They knocked and knocked but could not get in.

It rained and rained and kept raining. The ark rocked and rolled back and forth on the sea that was created by the rain.

They had everything they needed on the ark to last them forty days and forty nights. People were screaming, "Help!" "Help us!" "Save us!" But it was too late.

It continued to rain just as God said it would. All life that was not on the ark had drowned from the flood of the rain.

It rained in the daytime and at nighttime without ceasing; without slowing up, the rain came down hard. The animals enjoyed the rain falling on them as it poured down from heaven.

There was a great downpour. God released the rain, and the floodwaters came on earth. In the six hundredth year of Noah's life, on the seventeenth day of the second month, on the same day all the fountains of the great deep, it rained on the earth and the windows and floodgates of the heavens were opened.

The waters prevailed so greatly and were so mighty and overwhelming on the earth that all the high mountains everywhere under the heavens were covered. God made the rainbow to remind Noah of the promise that He made to him that He would never destroy the world by water again.

Everyone on the dry land who was not on the ark, everything that once had breath had died. God wiped away every living thing. Only Noah and those on the ark remained alive. The waters covered the earth for 150 days and five months.

THE RAIN STOPPED

There was a quietness outside. No more storming, no more lightning, no more rain hitting against the roof and windows. It had stopped raining; it had been forty days.

After the forty days and forty nights of the nonstop raining, finally there were clear skies. No more rain. The sun was shining bright, and only eight people remained alive to recreate the whole world.

The ark landed on dry land on the mountains in Turkey. The waters continued to decrease until the tenth month; on the first day of the tenth month, the tops of the mountains were able to be seen.

God remembered Noah and his family and every living thing, all the animals that were with him in the ark. After 150 days, the waters diminished. After another forty days, Noah sent out a raven.

The raven flew here and there all around the earth seeking dry land. The raven did not find any dry land.

Then Noah opened the window of the ark and sent out a dove to see if the water lever had fallen below the surface of the land.

The dove flew from the window, just as the raven did, trying to find dry land on the earth. The dove flew here and there.

The dove flew and flew all around trying to find dry land, but no dry land could be found, no place on which to rest the sole of her foot, and she returned to Noah because the waters were still on earth.

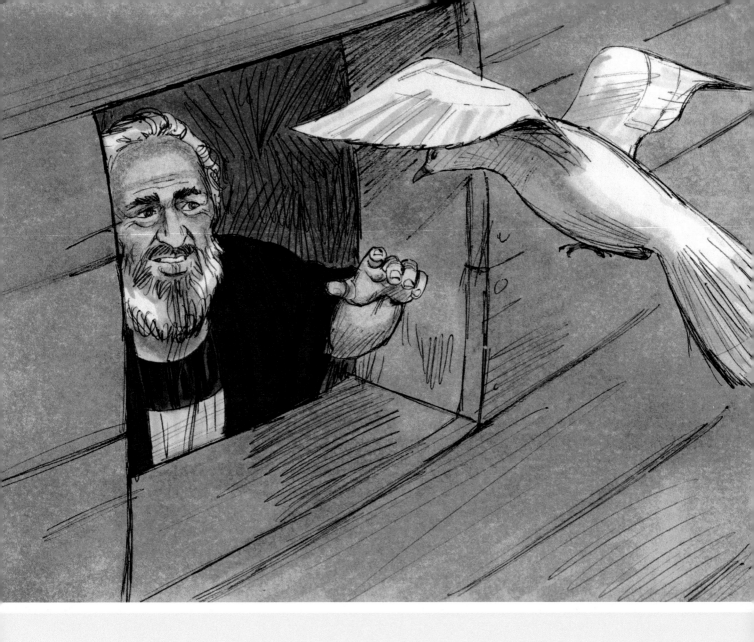

Noah stood in the window and saw the dove returning to the ark because there was no dry land for the dove. He reached out his hand and took the dove and brought her into the ark. Noah waited another seven days and again sent the dove out from the ark to search for dry land.

THE DOVE FINDS DRY LAND

The dove returned back to the ark in the evening, and there on her beak was a fresh olive leaf. So Noah knew that the water lever had subsided from the earth.

Noah waited another seven days and sent out the dove, but she did not return to him again because she found dry land on the earth.

Noah was 601 years old. Noah and his family and all the animals exited the ark onto dry land for the first time after the flood.

On the twenty-seventh day of the second month, the land was entirely dry. God spoke to Noah, saying, "Go out of the ark—you and your wife and you sons and their wives with you."

God told Noah to bring out every living thing from all flesh—birds and animals and every crawling thing that crawls on the earth—that they may breed abundantly and be fruitful and multiply on the earth.

Noah built an altar to the Lord and took of every ceremonially clean animal and every clean bird and offered burnt offerings on the altar.

The Lord smelled the pleasing aroma, a soothing satisfying scent, and the Lord said to Himself, "I will never again curse the ground because of man for the intent strong inclination—desire of man's heart is wicked from his youth, and I will never again destroy every living thing as I have done."

Then He said, "While the earth remains, seedtime and harvest, cold and heat, winter and summer, and day and night shall not cease."

THE RAINBOW COVENANT

God blessed Noah and his sons and said to them, "Be fruitful and multiply and fill the earth. Every animal of the land and every bird of the air, or that moves on the ground and in the sea are given into your hand.

The Lord told Noah, "Every moving thing that lives shall be food for you. I give you everything, as I give you the green plants and vegetables.

God spoke to Noah and his sons with him, saying, "Now behold, I am establishing My covenant-binding agreement, solemn promise with you and with your descendants after you and with every living creature that is with you—the birds, the livestock, and the wild animals of the earth along with you.

Then He told Noah and his sons, "Everything that comes out of the ark—every living creature of the earth, I will establish My covenant with you: never again shall all flesh be cut off by the water of a flood, nor shall there ever again be a flood to destroy and ruin the earth."

God said, "This is the token visible symbol—memorial of the solemn covenant that I am making between Me and you and every living creature that is with you and every living thing for all generations.

I set My rainbow in the clouds, and it shall be a sign of a covenant between Me and the earth. It shall come about when I bring clouds over the earth that the rainbow shall be seen in the clouds, and I will compassionately remember My covenant, which is between Me and you and every living creature."

Noah and his three sons—Shem, Ham, and Japheth—began to repopulate the earth. Upon these three men, the whole earth was populated. Ham would become the father of Canaan.

THE END

Printed in the United States
by Baker & Taylor Publisher Services